contraband
of hoopoe

BOOKS IN POLISH:

Furkot, Studium Press, Kraków, Poland, 2003
Sopiłki, Fraza Press, Rzeszów, Poland, 2009

BOOKS IN ENGLISH:

Strata, Emergency Press, New York, 2011

contraband
of hoopoe
ewa chrusciel

OMNIDAWN PUBLISHING
RICHMOND, CALIFORNIA
2014

Cover art: Julie Püttgen, *Cloudmapping: Conference of the Birds*, 2008.
Gouache, watercolor, and pencil, 12 × 16 in.

Book cover & interior design by Cassandra Smith

Offset printed in the United States
by Edwards Brothers Malloy, Ann Arbor, Michigan
On 55# Enviro Natural 100% Recycled 100% PCW
Acid Free Archival Quality FSC Certified Paper
with Rainbow FSC Certified Colored End Papers

Library of Congress Cataloging-in-Publication Data

Chrusciel, Ewa.
  [Poems. Selections]
  Contraband of hoopoe / Ewa Chrusciel.
    pages cm
  ISBN 978-1-890650-99-5 (pbk. : alk. paper)
  I. Title.
  PS3603.H78A6 2014
  811'.6--dc23

                                        2014013751

Published by Omnidawn Publishing, Richmond, California
www.omnidawn.com (510) 237-5472 (800) 792-4957
          10 9 8 7 6 5 4 3 2 1
          ISBN: 978-1-890650-99-5

To my parents

Contents

The past is a foreign country: they do things differently there.

A. P. Hartley

Can you feel the apparition? The hoopoe's wings beat under my blouse. The sound *udud udud udud* is tearing from my nipples: Pagan pole dancing, my breasts have Tourette's syndrome. My breasts are in flux as if singing church hymns kneeling down, standing up, kneeling down. I have to stop and soothe them with new lullabies.

The hoopoe is the dybbuk messenger chattering under my bra. This action is not unprecedented. King Solomon sent the hoopoe across the oceans to the Queen of Sheba to urge her with religion. Pliny said nothing about the hoopoe. On the other hand, Kircher in his Collegio Romano had a hoopoe in his collection of skeletons among bones of eagles, magpies, thrushes, and a Brazilian monkey.

My valley of deprivation, my cloud of unknowing, pray for me *Upupa epops*. Convert me back to wonder. Cure my heart of such morbid desires to come home. It is you who take me across ocean, just as he once took all the world's birds on a pilgrimage to Simurgh. To a new land where jays are not jaded and finches do not fling seeds at small children.

When I cross the border, I start hiccupping. The officer stares at my nipples. I carry wonder inside me. I bring abundance. I stir the wings within him.

I buy a sausage at the airport before I leave Poland. Kiełbaska, kiełbasa, kabanos, kabanosik. This, my transcontinental dowry. The sacrificial baby of my tongue. Foreign gods hover over us. If God lets my sausage in, I will eat it like a saint wreathed in incense, circle a table with Gregorian chants. *Folkberg* variations. The baggage carousel spurts my luggage out. With an air of conspiracy, I transfer this sausage from my carry-on into checked luggage. I look around. I pray for my sausage while I move towards customs. The Angelus trickles. The Angelus salivates. St. George is about to put his spear through a sizzling dragon. My luggage goes through a "sausage scan." Can an old sausage be born young again? The officer pulls me aside. The officer holds my sausage to the light. His babushka trophy. "It's a sealed sausage." I declare with pride. I've brought a new species. "But you declared: no meats," the officer says. "Sealed Sausage is not a meat!" "Sealed sausage is a sealed sausage!" I say, as the guardian angels of my sealed sausage swarm under the investigation light. The officer blinks when I repeat with determination: "A sealed sausage is a sealed sausage." He looks blinded. My hypnotic alliteration throws him back into the waters of his childhood where eels jiggle Scottish dances. Oh, sweet detained sausage. Saint of arrests, pray for us. May my new species have mercy on us. Escape at the borders. Oh, oven bird, whose migratory song is a sausage a sausage a sausage. Dear sausage of martyrs. Sealed patriarch. Let the Virgin Liberty swallow it.

We take the turf with us. We take the dirt with us. We smuggle mortality. We smuggle the dust. We carry the clay. We make the words out of little clumps of earth where all the word-roots of words are. Where the lines of poems spring from. Isn't it bacteria that turned the water into wine? *To thy high requiem become a sod.* Scatological belongings, we transmit literature through toilets. The turf is soaked with the metaphors of our country. The turf translates bones, not to be broken. The gas of our ancestors. It is a bomb. It sizzles. Do you see a mulberry tree in a mustard seed? We will cover the seed with our soil. We will transplant the seeds in rows 12 inches apart.

The first time we went to Bulgaria with our parents it was 1978. There was no toilet paper in Polish shops. What is humanity without a decent roll of toilet paper? Every time I saw the toilet paper, I would roll it secretly. I wanted to bring some luxury home. In Western countries there was paper, but no truth to write on it. We knew the truth, but had no paper. No paper to wipe off the system. We carried it like a turf on our asses. What is the culture that cannot regenerate itself by healthy digestion? This is where we beheld the system. Not enough toilet paper to relieve our attitude. There is no good literature without good toilet paper.

Ellis I

they carried boxes they carry goose feathers they carried comforters
they carried Bibles they carried candlesticks they carry pillows they
carry voids and maps they carried blue barrels of sadness
they carry a live goat they carried barrels of pickles they carry a honey-
moon dress they carry tweezers they carried pins they carried buttons
they carried crucifixes they carry hand-painted Easter eggs they carried
The Book of Common Prayer they carry pocketknives they carried tears
they carry sewing machines they carry donkey shoes for good luck
they carried luminous & dark *duende* they carried children
they carry accordions they carried ceramic pipes they carry fears
they carry sheets they carry wurst and pretzels, doughnuts,
"beygals," "knishes," they carry the distance from what they loved
the most they carried vowels and consonants they carried spices and intersections
they carried bed pillows they carry bedspreads they carried towels they carry
mangled boards they carried rolling pins they carry a spice shaker
they carry their grief into a hundredfold of grief they carry
their hopes into a hundredfold of hope

He wraps each hummingbird in cloth. They look like newborn babies. He sews each pouch into the inside of his underwear. He heads for the Rochambeau airport in Cayenne. What are the true desires in this disguise? The man did not know that hummingbirds calculate their own rates of return. The man did not know that bird means penis in some languages. *Horror vacui*? How many small birds can one have in his underwear? Do you see a mulberry tree in a mustard seed? Smuggling comes from a species of restlessness. It is a small creature. It promises intensity. It has a lingering nature. It likes to be wrapped in paper or plastic. It likes hiding places. It stirs its wings, stretches in flight. A haul of hummingbirds in his underwear.

We are hordes of Tartar cheeks, the ruthless blood of ancestors. We ripple. We spread halos. We carry Genghis Khan. We plunder. We swirl in wakes. We proliferate robust blushes. We bolt downhill, the light streaming through our spokes. We swell. We carry abysses. The birds on stilts in fields of rye greet us in midflight. With Heaven's aid we will conquer a huge empire. We gather into our bosom your wives and daughters. We store oranges and plums in our cheeks. We are contagious. We carry yellow secrets. We smell of the vast steppes. We plant the courtyards of Kublai Khan. Inside us the grand khan takes you on a horse ride. A small leopard carried on a horse's back. On the twenty-eighth day of the moon in August, the astrologers scatter the milk from mares as an offering to all the spirits. We carry the feather of a giant bird rukh. The most fantastical truths can be smuggled only through the windy labyrinths of our body's cavities.

Do you read the hoopoe or are you being read by the hoopoe? Do you penetrate the mystery of feathers in feathers? The hoopoe brings silence to the world of noises. Each noise has an "I" imprinted on it and each "I" is galloping somewhere. Each "I" is riding its motorcycle. Each "I" inhabits space by making tunnels. The hoopoe is a Sufi mystic who leads all the world's birds on a pilgrimage to encounter Simurgh, the ultimate Mystery. But the birds steep in attachments and try to smuggle them on their journey. That weighs on their feathers. The Nightingale smuggles love for a Rose. The Parrot wants to take the cage. The Duck smuggles water. The Partridge, precious stones. The Heron—the whole sea. The Owl—treasures. But the hoopoe says: "So long as we do not die to ourselves, we shall never be free." The hoopoe says: "For how can you remain the master of yourself if you follow your likes and dislikes?" The hoopoe says: "Set upon your Way, for you are not an almond, you are only the shell." The hoopoe smuggles you into yourselves. The hoopoe smuggled Solomon into Sheba. He is the courier of wisdom. Correspondent between false infinities and Infinity itself.

Smuggling's disruption: the airport door hangs ajar through which ghosts and solid apparitions will sneak out and march like little soldiers into new frontiers. The music of smuggling is jazz, is improvisation, only possible due to arduous preparatory practices.

The Lascaux Man did not only imitate the world of nature—he painted imaginary horned beings and other mysterious semianimal lifeness. He transgressed. He smuggled the excess. He carried the third space. Even Aristotle's closural *mimesis* gives in to openings through *deus ex eachina*, epiphanic *catharsis* and, on a linguistic level, metaphors.

Joyce was a smuggler of identities. Evanescences. Which flicker. In a letter to his brother Stanislaus, Joyce catalogued some of his favorites. He was a cocaine addict, an Austrian spy, the founder of *dadaism*, and a Bolshevik propagandist. James Gavin writes that for Joyce "intrigue and peril meant avoiding the landlord on rent day."

E. D. smuggled Longfellow and Jane Eyre. Her father Edward thought contemporary books would joggle her mind. So she would hide them under the laurel bush or under the piano. What do we smuggle of her into posterity? Letters she asked to have burned after her death. A Parisian chocolate wrapper with her poem on it. A lock of her red hair. Slip of paper with a little tomb sketched on the back. 3-cent stamp. A coconut cake recipe. Two daguerreotypes. Relics of her rebuses which concealed desires and freckles.

Smuggling is a big Kinder Surprise. It is a nesting doll. It is *pentimento*. It is a door ajar.

There is no life for them in the old Continent, these pigeons called rats. They have acquired the wrong reputation. They coo their litanies. They sing to the faces of their landlords. They congregate on balconies to interfere with Sunday hymns. The pigeons are better worshippers, truer. We were told to take sticks and beat these white dybbuks. One neighbor had a pistol. I was told to hit them. Rustling of their wings in takeoff. Masters of survival and telepathy. What illness springs from a lost place? Blood changes into water. They nest on my head. My wig becomes their cradle, a boat. I am crossing the borders with this coiffure of feathers. They need to have a new beginning; re-winging. All the peace of the world perches on my head. I take two more and jam them in between my tights. I walk funny. I wobble. The stewardess offers me a wheelchair. I cross borders cooing. The officer wonders if I am medicated. No one leaves without a mission. I carry the legions of white feathers. Tiny terrorists flutter in the air.

Ellis II

Albert Sabin, a pauper from Białystok carries a live virus, the vaccine that eliminated polio from the United States. Khalil Gibran, an Arab, carries the viruses of poetry with him and *The Prophet*. Isaac Asimov carries measles with him, as well as *Pebbles in the Sky* and *The Naked Sun*. Igor Sikorsky carries helicopters. Pola Negri carries stars. Frank Capra carries *The Strong Man*, *Ladies of Leisure*, *Lost Horizon*, *Arsenic and Old Lace*, *You Can't Take It with You*. Pearl Primus carries dances and leaps. Lilly Daché carries chic chapeaus. Anna Yezierska carries *Hungry Hearts*, *Bread Givers*, *Salome of the Tenements*, and *Children of Loneliness*. Alfred Levitt carries *Paysage Provençal* and *Growth and Fruition*. Henry Roth carries *Mercy of a Rude Stream* and *Call It Sleep*. Arshile Gorky carries *The Artist's Mother*, *Nighttime, Nostalgia, Enigma*, and *Agony*.

Jan Karski, a Polish Catholic, dresses as a Jew to smuggle evidence from the ghetto. He takes with him his photographic memory. Light bleeds and x-rays. He carries swooning eyes. He carries the dybbuks in the pores of his skin. In his pockets. The clouds of children. The porous streets, the ditches and sewers carry them. Pebbles of children in his mouth. These stones were feathers first. Red hair, feet of swallows. Swollen crosses. Red flicks. What trickles out of a smuggler's mouth? These children shrink into ripples. They trickle out of sewers into the other side, into their Christian names. They tap the earth. They are eggshells. He carries them to the land where honey and milk flow down the streets. He carries these dybbuks to the White House. In his palm their squawks and whimpers. He places his palm in Roosevelt's palm. His ruffled feet meet Roosevelt's feet leaning on a table. The swallows trickle out of Karski's mouth. The smoke of Roosevelt's cigarettes swallows the charcoal lines. Roosevelt in his swallow-tailed coat waits. His feet rock away the crucifixions. The smuggled Jews are noted down on the invisible 16th page of the *New York Times*. Invisible wrinkles on the page. A tree gets planted in his name in Jerusalem. Both Karski and the tree take the vow of silence.

I carry the twigs of the dead tree from my home street in Kraków as spoons. Into a bedding of combs. While muscular men with saws sing their funerals. The twigs wheeze. They wail. The spoons pebble my new kitchen. A spoon perches in my heart recurrently. An owl, it scoops out faces at dusks. Mere puffs of feathers. The hills palpitate. As tails of deer flash. And light the candles. In what meadows. In what dusks. Where does that tree reside? The hummingbird darts through the rhododendron. The spoons pebble into words. And then into incense. In shoals of what other trees. I see them congregating on the highway. On another continent. In glow of red burst into psalms.

It hides in between the birches. It flickers. Hide-and-seek. How mystery winks. An apparition of deer. The candle of his tail back into dark. *The chinks in the forest.* The winks of light into zebras on the forest floor. Stripes undulate into currents. Trees smuggle the Sacred. But the souls leap into leaves, bark, wrinkles, fissures, stalks, husks. The trees, the smugglers of cemeteries with rings of psalms. They compete with children on All Souls' Day. From many winged seeds the taproots hum the *Book of Hours.* They dart like finches. There is no way to fix them. They hide in cracks and whispers. They listen. To what is not. They are brief and violent. They unconceal. They burst forth. Theirs is unveiling. They will light the continent for me. Tigers of wrath and light. The trees are not without kaddish. Mimosas, Pagodas, Figs, and Rowans. The soul composed of very small atoms produces small dream-stations.

Can one smuggle the language of an oak—harsh, robust, sturdy? An underworld of roots? Can one smuggle 47 thousand vowels and consonants stemming and sprouting from the root of one tree? *If we go down into ourselves we find that we possess exactly what we desire.* Smuggling is a journey, not a miracle. Noah was a smuggler. He carried thirsty cicada. He shipped the sacraments. The fish rippled under his feet. In his pockets, litanies of eels. His prayers blossomed into fins. Water had lungs and memory. Noah smuggled the blue-footed booby who later settled on the Galápagos Islands. The real smuggler sorts out his catch.

Ellis III

She takes a birch twig whisk. An x-ray of her land. For stirring butter,
porridge, gravy. Birches make underground passages. They make
new universes. They shed speckled skins. She takes the largest living
organism. She carves new tastes into them. They comb the paths to
new homes. They stretch for acres and seas. They shoot roots into
clay dishes, into burlap floors. They tangle and mesh into windows.
They whisk the curtain frills. They *unleave*. Winged forks from inside
explode, scatter new letters into the air. They beat new wings. They
take off. A bird of paradise out of the birch tweaks. 47 thousand stems
from one root. Do you see a mulberry tree in a mustard seed?

A bird of paradise flies out of his bag at the Los Angeles airport. It is 2010. A bird of God swishes his tail and shakes his head, gaping at the customs officer. An opera version of a crow. A cousin of a jay in figure-skating costumes. Said to never fly except when the wind blows. In 1522 stowed in the cargo holds in Magellan's ship, *Victoria*, a dozen dead birds of paradise as a gift from Sultan of Bacan for the King of Spain. Now he slides alive out of a twenty-first-century salvage bag. A firework, or maybe a meteor, smuggles immortality into the airport. The golden-feathered bird which never lands and feeds on dew. To attract the bird, Aru hunters would rub the wax from their ear on the tree trunk. If bird in some language stands for penis, what does a Bird of God stand for? Phallic exaggeration? Pollinator of the evanescence? Oh, bird of paradise spread your ballerina cape, swish your tail and prank up the air. The airport prays in volcanic humming.

Noah smuggled a blue-footed booby in his resin boat. But how was infinity smuggled in the blue feet of the booby? It crouched in his webbed feet and chanted madrigals. Booby, you strut your blue feet in the air and point the human species to the sky. No smuggler can get hold of your blueness. You are the incarnation of the sky. Your feet are the metonymies. You cover your chicks with your blueness. Your feet are the blueprints of God's infancy. How you waddle and wiggle them in the air. A celestial clown you are, booby. An aristocrat of blue and blue and blue.

The hoopoe says:

When you have the ocean why will you seek a drop of evening dew?

In his suitcase fifty rare orchids, blooming. He smuggles excess. He is bringing pollen grains, stamens, and ovaries. To be permanently aloft, to transgress. The orchid, once a son of a satyr and a nymph, morphed into a plant. The Greek name of the orchid is "testicle." *Horror vacui.*

When asked if he has anything else illegal, he replies: "Yes, I've got monkeys in my pants."

Ellis IV

Nathan Solomon takes a quilt and a pillow beater. Polish highlanders made one out of a tree. A pillow beater is a miniature palm. He beats his linens every Friday morning in preparation for the Sabbath.

It is January 1923, the Sabbath.

She takes three cupping glasses. The way her mother placed them heated on her chest and back to draw infection out. To carry glass candles on your back. Little moons burning. Tiny spheres. Circumferences. New globes. To be under the bell jar.

John Winthrop writes to his wife to bring eggs put up in salt or ground malt, butter, oatmeal, peas, and fruits. "Be sure to be warmed-clothed and have a store of fresh provisions."
It is 1630.

She takes a copper pot to make gefilte fish. She even has *Fiscus* in her last name. She will remain faithful to her fish. But now the fish scaled into a tiger fish, a butterfly loach, a flying fish, a snowflake moray eel, a cowfish, a baby whale, a black knife fish. They carry the fins of a siren. They sing. They summon. They flap and flip. They jingle. They giggle. They quiver. They swirl in wakes. The new land has a myriad of minnows. The acrobats of the new seas open their dazzling fins.

Hippocrates recommended consuming deer penis to resolve sexual difficulties. Some women in Taiwan used to eat it during pregnancy to make the mother and child stronger. To fatten them. There are a bunch of us now, each smuggling a deer penis. We will bless the new country with virility. The dwarf woman is using it as a cane. She is limping. Her daughter has a wooden Pinocchio toy with her. Deer penis serves as his nose. A grandma can hang her shopping bag on it. Children will use it as a bridge in the new country when they cross the river. We will serve it in a large jar to all special guests as a delicacy. We will open a mainland restaurant. It is a gift of sacrifice. Taken from the deer while he is still alive. Then roasted and dried in the sun while the deer looks on. We will soak it in alcohol and serve it as penis wine. We will recommend it for athletic injuries. Two hundred dollars per liter. At home, it will warm us. It will multiply us. What are the true desires in this disguise? Deer is a sacred noun. It is the apparition of Beauty. *Horror vacui.* Catching the joy as it flies.

Smuggling has to do with metonymies. Metonymies assure us we have nutshells. Metonymies assure us we have eggshells. The fragment, the part of a greater whole, residing in the spiritual realm. Metonymies are centrifugal. They dwell in particulars, peripheries. They have something to do with myopic perception. Metonymies are easier to smuggle. Smugglers do not like throwing away the cheese wrappers and glass jars from their country, as they stand for something bigger. Smugglers yearn for the absent whole. Smuggling is both the attachment and the red herring. It is a condensation of departure. It supplies associations. Just like metonymy, it has to do with compression. It bodies forth lack. It speaks of insufficiency. It is the desire to restore the subject to its predicate. It is a deferral of leaving. It is a relationship of ship to sail. We can take in the sail. Nobody wants to go with empty hands. Smuggling shortens the distance in between.

Litany of Confiscation

Animal Head of Unknown Origin – defend us

Beanie Babies – feed us

Belts – embrace us

Bird's Nest – root us

Bird Corpse – spare us

Bongs – stone us

Butterflies of Prohibition – flutter grace on us

Candy Made from Animals – sweeten smuggled beasts in us

Cashier Checks – bring us prosperity

Chestnuts – crisp us

Chicken Feet – don't leap before you hatch

Chicken Miscellaneous – sustain us

Cock Fertility Tablets – sex us up

Cow Urine – cure us

Cuban Cigars – envelop us in invisibility

Deer Antlers – protect us

Deer Blood – heal us

Deer Penis – cure our uncertainties

Deer Tongue – stick out at our enemies

Eggshells – let us walk carefully

Ginkgo Nuts – whisper of Permian Oceans

Khat – hypnotize us

Kinder Surprise – snuggle us

Leaves – rustle in us

Lighter – blind the officers of prohibition

Mombins – entertain us

Moon Cakes – taste us

Nesting Dolls – coil us

Oca – do whatever you want for us
Onions – cry officers' eyes out
Palm Fruit – sing of our victory
Pickled Mango – giggle at us
Pigeon Tablets – unpack cooing for us
Seeds – germinate us
Snails – coil us
Whole Duck – quack us
Thirteen Bottles of Overproof Rum – frolic in us
Tree Bark – layer us

His pockets smell of vast steppes, roots, mosses, lichens. He carries the hair of musk ox from Greenland. He is bringing metonymies. He will give it to a girl, Autumn, who loves the musk ox. They will make a scarf or spend the afternoon playing with the hair. He cannot take the eight-hundred-pound bull who roars, swings its head and paws the ground. Musk oxen in defense form a tight circle, a ring or a crescent moon. Now in his car he is carrying the plastic grocery bag full of musk ox hair. What illness springs from lost hair? *Horror vacui?* People clip their children's hair. My mother trimmed my hair when the moon was full. Musk oxen's hair is a protector. It reaches to the ground. It is a curtain and a cooler. He is taking musk oxen back to their migratory place twenty thousand years ago. Sea turtles migrate far into the ocean only to return to the same beach where they were born. A single grain of sand has its mountain to go back to.

Before I leave for America, my dad comes to the airport with a dish of *pierogi*. He entices me to eat them. His way of making sure I smuggle the whole of Poland in my belly. I am pregnant with Polish wheat, with poppies and goats. To feed others is to say "I love you." Do not die. I sustain you. I give you a piece of my earth. The long tread of a farmer in a field? Furrows and raw wind? The hidden nerves inside each loaf? How this bread whispers. It rustles and creaks. A walk in the woods, the kneading and molding of your hands.

Ellis V

Dieticians in the early 20th century discouraged Hungarian, Polish, Jewish children from eating dill pickles (with their supposedly negative impact on the urinary tract). Bertha Wood deplored the sour and pickled flavors and the rich foods popular among Eastern Europeans & Jews: these caused "irritation," she argued, rendering "assimilation more difficult" in a people already so "emotional" that they went too often to their doctors.

My grandmother makes *bigos* for me. It is in a jar, in a bottle that will be washed ashore on the new lands. *Bigos* carries the smell of Lithuanian woods and hunters. A Lithuanian Grand Duke who became the Polish king Władysław Jagiełło in 1385 supposedly served *bigos* to his hunting-party guests. *Bigos* of two nations. The transgression of borders. *Bigos* was for robust, sturdy men. *Bigos* is made of cabbage and sauerkraut, mushrooms, wine and meat. "What a *bigos*" means metaphorically "confusion," "big mess" or "trouble" in Polish. However, Polish linguists trace the word *bigos* to a German rather than Lithuanian origin. It derives from the past participle *begossen* of a German verb meaning "to douse." The confusion of customs. The liquidation of borders.

I smuggle her hula hoop skirts. Queen of the oven and drawers
stuffed with candy. Hysteric who chased us with hunks of bread

upholstered in honey. Czarina of household complaints, cicada of suitors,
hippo of hypochondria, curator of covert farts.
Countess of church bazaars. My posthumous bride
now interred in a vat of poppy seeds:
Babushka. Grandma of flower pots dressed up in gold foil:

How can I find you again
in the bog of this world?

In 1950 Andrzej L smuggled forty-five thousand razor blades on his way back from a sport contest. A director of a Silesian factory smuggled one hundred and fourteen silk scarves. A writer, Janusz Głowacki, reminisces about smuggling porcelain vases from Poland to Czechoslovakia, where they sold well. Women's underwear, watches, cigarettes… In the trains from Warsaw to Vienna, there were hiding places under the seats. Austrian accomplices would put the goods ordered by mail or phone there. The whole country changed into a Gigantic Contraband. Our parents were smugglers of sweets mostly. Every time we traveled in our Fiat to Czechoslovakia, we would buy chocolate and gummy bears. Now, whenever I travel from state to state, at the gas station and the airports I buy a pack of gummy bears. Gummy bears, the patron saints of contraband.

Prayer before Flight

Storks bring babies and wealth.
Storks build their nests on electricity poles
along the highways in Poland.
To take a muster of storks.
To carry a phalanx of storks on my shoulders.
White, fluttering knapsack.
I want to carry a pole with a stork, a good pilgrim.
White apparition in the air.
To soar on stork's wings.
What illness springs from a lost place?
In Aristophanes, grown-up storks support their parents
by migrating elsewhere and conducting warfare.
Storks, *pelargos*, were cousins of indigenous Greeks, *Pelasgians*.
The stork is Odysseus disguised as a wild orchid.
Storks are linguistic cousins of the sea, *pelagos*.
The sea leaps its letters in the air.

1974. An old man holds a votive candle at the Polish-Ukrainian border. An ancient wax figure. His skin, a yellow paraffin. He came to Poland to get the candle for his grave. The religious votives are unattainable under the regime in Ukraine. The candle, a prayer clasped in his hands. He carries the unspoken Resurrection. Kitchen and the Apocalypse. The officer pulls the candle out of his hand and tosses it into the garbage can. Darkness, his candle. The dogwoods grow in silence. Who is the burning man? How can you know a candle from a moth? What illness springs from a lost place? Trees clasp their fiery hands. I smuggle a smoke film, ghosting. I want to carry him to the Mother of Exiles. To her beacon hand, a glowing candle. Your huddled masses yearning to breathe free. She lifts her candle beside the golden door. A polycandela. A drumming station. The intensity of the instance burns. A fire rises above his hands.

All Souls' Poem

We smuggled the souls out
of cemeteries. The offerings
of celibate bees on the altar,
the souls flamed in beeswax candles.

We scooped them out of circular rims,
from liquid pools we fished them
with our fingers, to seal them
into silhouettes.

We held the saints and sinners.
We played dolls with them in tiny
village theatres. We coated them
on cold Polish November days.

We molded them in our hands.
We mingled them.
We pinched them.

The many figures of wax
softening, dripping down
our fingers, tapping the earth.

A procession of novenas, flames
meandered through the graves
and chrysanthemums rose

Ellis VI

Ann Andersen from Denmark takes a sheet used only during deliveries. Her sheet, a shroud of the womb. It springs birth. It is her legacy. She will show it to her new doctor. It produces a loud shushing noise. The blood pulses through white cotton. The sheet carries a crying infant. It will cover empty avenues and streets. It populates.

The Mirelovitz Family takes with them a mandolin, photographs, two drinking glasses, and three children. They tie all these in bundles while fleeing Vilnius. It is 1909. Pogroms against Jews.

Helena Bastedo puts on herself petticoats, dresses, sweaters, coats. She is huge. She carries the guardian angels of her clothes. She is a walking wardrobe.

The Perdikis Family from Cyprus takes with them a doily, a shawl, an icon of St. George killing a dragon, a child's ebony cane, a diploma from a Boy Scout Troop, an icon of St. Helen, a wooden flask, pieces of coral from waters around Larnaca.

Prayer on the Runway

I take snowflakes magnified by grace. I put them in jars. Stellar dendrites, crystal partitions, specks of sparks. They swirl in myriad wakes. White anarchy of feathers. Species of sacred flurries. Miniature albatrosses in disguise. The snow glistens, it is my flashlight. I cut through crowds of foreign solitudes. I glide through space and slopes. Meandering white brides. The frills and flounces of woods. A flock of Dominican monks on skis. Dervishes unveiling. Snow clasps its hands in prayer. Splashing litanies of lifts and turns. The ceremonies of *kristianias*. Plowing the fields of snow. Pollinating snow-lilies into powder.

White ptarmigans flutter their chants of feathers. Lift off. In what image.

I was six and I did not entertain the thought of sharing my chewing gums. When a Romanian approached our car on our way to the Bulgarian seaside and asked for chewing gum, I responded: "We have them, but you would not know how to chew them." The woman got so offended she spat on our car. For Poles, chewing gum symbolized the West, a development. An old Romanian seemed too poor and backwards for chewing gum. The wife's old tale said that the swallowed gum would remain in a human's stomach for up to seven years. To swallow a gum meant no progress. It was my pride not to swallow one. Yet the chewing gum belonged to the old generations. The chewing gum was already known in the Neolithic Period. It was a birch bark tar. Ancient Aztecs used Manilkara chicle. The American Indians chewed the resin from sap of spruce trees. Did the West colonize chewing gum?

1980. I am 8. Some kids from the Ukraine visit us. They ask us for
holy pictures. Any items of faith are forbidden in Ukraine. I give them
the pictures of Holy Mary carrying baby Jesus. St. Joseph, the guardian
of poverty. They hide them in their cameras. Mary and her most sacred
spouse are squeezed inside the box, x-rayed. They are reading *Alice
in Wonderland.* The space contracts. The space of reference merges
and becomes as thin as the photographic plate. They are developing
the film, the saints. The kids carry the saints on their tiny shoulders.
What do saints carry? St. Theresa carries roses. St. Catherine carries
the wheel. St. Christopher carries new maps, new avenues. John of
the Cross carries the dark night of unknowing. St. Francis carries
animals. He helps me carry the hoopoes, pigeons, and hedgehogs. He
pacifies the snakes under my chest. Padre Pio carries stigmata. Saints
transgress the Law of Customs. They smuggle wonder into infinity.
The desire to never settle for less.

Prayer in Midflight

I carry the feet of a mystic on my neck.
The cloud of unknowing.
There is a face within my face.
A sacred heron.
Eikon is being engraved there
through pebbling.
Indwelling of the saint.
I delineate the circles.
The strokes, continuous.
We carry the Light with us.
Our faces, each—an icon,
translucent layers of color.
Boundaries delineate the sacred.
The sacred hides in crossings,
intercessions, relics of belongings.
Relics of kitchens and toilets,
hanging over new precipices.

Ellis VII

What did the Matrimonial Ship carry?
Two hundred and thirty-one Picture Brides with the photographs
of their future husbands.

The inner soles of brides' shoes lined with the eggshells. They walk
with porcelain attention. They do not want to mangle their alphabets.
What profit would they have, if they were to gain the whole world and
lose their broken selves?

What did coffin ships bring?
Dead boy lice dead girl lice dead grandma lice dead grandpa lice
dead bodies lice dead lice dead vermin dead vermin dead vermin.

I smuggle dead brides. I smuggle an Albanian soldier. I smuggle the Guadalupe Madonna. I smuggle a Turkish bank guard. I smuggle Romanian shepherds. I smuggle Sikhs from India. I smuggle a rabbi. I smuggle babushkas. I smuggle Italian pipers. I smuggle a Russian giant. I smuggle Gypsies. I smuggle orphans. I smuggle microcephalics. I carry their ashes. I carry their vermin. I carry their secrets. I carry their feet. I carry their elbows. I carry their rosy cheeks. I carry their pale corpses. I carry roses and tulips. I carry voids and maps, blue barrels, sandpipers obsessing on the beach. Neurons and rhododendrons. Ageratum on Shelburne Falls Bridge. Virginia creepers. Seals and amulets, cuneiform wedges. Nursing Virgins flanked by two angels. Quay Brothers. Streets of Crocodiles. Green papayas. With each worn-out circumference we gain one more road, coterminous with its longing. And a distance from what we love the most. Lascaux painters toiled in darkness and saw only parts of their work flicker. Lorca's ant gave its life for the moment of astonishment. Smuggling will not seal the broken vases. It will make your grief one hundredfold, and carry it into other griefs.

Prayer

The Large Blue Dress took Matisse endless versions,
repeated rubbings out of
the areas of paint, etching
sinuous lines—

Until putrid matter is purity,
the seawater interacts with oceanic crust
of scratching colors,
until the light bleeds
into blue and blue and not blue
in its infinities.

On the volcanic Azorean islands,
locals make tiny flowers and nativity scenes
out of scales of fish,
their layered rings reveal their age.

Each canvas, a scale, a scalloped rock
unveils light years of porousness
until blue beads form a rosary.

Black basalt accepts drafts,
flutings, lineations, missing
cavities, strata, which
in my language means
loss.

Smuggling is translation. Between a subject and an object. Between an idea and reality. Between reality and a shadow. Between a pronoun and an imperative. It is—for those who are unable to let go—nesting in two places at once. It is a yearning for bilocation. Some Christians were adept at it. St. Anthony of Padua, St. Ambrose of Milan, St. Severus of Ravenna, and Padre Pio of Italy. Both translation and smuggling come from longing for presence. From a loss. They speak of insufficiency of one life, one language. Yet insufficiency to express what is ineffable saves us from idolatry.

Irena Sendler gets permission to work in the Warsaw Ghetto as a plumber. She smuggles babies in her toolbox and carries larger children in her sack out of the Warsaw ghetto. Her dog knows when to bark to muffle the sounds of the crying children when Nazi soldiers are near. She carries the shrunk pebbles in wheelbarrows. Two thousand six hundred and thirty-five children ripple out of the Ghetto. She is small and plump like a donut. Through the gutters, through the tunnels, through the fissures blind moles dig their signs. Esther, Ezer, Aaron, Abigail, Becca, Imla will need to change their names and wrench their parents out of their palms. She buries their names in the jar. The names wriggle. The homunculi. The microscopic seahorses. Sendler eventually gets caught & tortured. I use here an ampersand to remember her wrenched body. In a sealed mouth. In an hourglass. She is a holy icon. Sendler gets nominated for the Nobel Peace Prize along with Al Gore, a smuggler of trees.

Ellis VIII

All of these tied in bundles and knots tied endlessly around the
bundles knots and knots encumbered by their luggage a small black
suitcase with Svenska—handmade by a Finnish immigrant in 1916.
They carry lice and vermin. The flocks of squawking gulls. Native
Americans called this island a Kioshk, Gull Island. Health certificate
between their beaks. For the Dutch fishermen it was Oyster Island,
Gibbet Island where a wayward sailor was hanged. Buttonhooks now
hang out of their eyes. Bundles and crucifixes hang on their shoulders.
In negative carriers. They carry luminous and dark *duende*. A Pole cuts
himself on the ship while shaving. The officer marks him with white
chalk on the face. He is denied entry. Words also arrive with their
bundles.

Nosadella the painter
moved the Angel first
from left to right
then made him vanish
with lead and white.
                    Incisions
        Ghost rays

The true annunciation happens
in the x-rays
in the wood grain, butterfly
wooden cleats, red wax seal,
three tapered wood dowels.

What remains?
A Crown
A watermark
Red chalk for her mantle
An enjambment
Haunted
by *pentimenti*,
Infrared

The Righteous among the Smugglers

Helena Adamska, Józef Adamski, Ferdynand Arczyński, Maria
Augustyn, Marian Blicharz, Weronika Blicharz, Józef Biesaga,
Tadeusz Bilewicz, Sabina Buczek, Wilhelm Buczek, Józefa Dadak,
Feliks Dangel, Maria Bobrowska, Stefan Chucherko, Eligia Dzielska,
Tadeusz Dzik, Helena Depa, Mirosław Dudek, Zofia Dudek, Tekla
Dzudziak, Władysław Druzkowiecki, Edwarda Dzielska, Teresa
Dietrich, Stefania Dobrowolska, Józef Elsner, Anna Fedorowicz,
Stefania Wilkosz-Filo, Maria Florek, Maria Gruca, Antonina Gebel,
Bolesław Gebel, Mirosława Gruszczyńska, Wanda Grabowska,
Bogusław Howil, Helena Howil, Czesława Jaksz, Zofia Jamioł, Jan
Jamro, Agata Janusz, Janina Klarman, Jan Krokowski, Artur Król,
Maria Klepacka, Lucia Kobylińska, Marta Kowalczyk-Jaksz, Salomea
Kowalczyk, Laura Kuzak, Maria Kot, Ryszard Kwiatek, Edward
Kubiczek, Aleksander Lau, Józef Lach, Maria Lipska, Stanisław
Matusz, ks. bp Albin Małysiak, Stefan Mika, Anna Milczanowska,
Władysława Miarczyńska, Maria Maciąg, Rozalia Natkaniec, Waleria
Niedzielska, Maria Nowak, Rudolf Nowak, Andrzej Pogonowski,
Bolesław Posławski, Antoni Reguła, Maria Reguła, Maria Barbara
Rudzka, Tadeusz Rewilak, Aniela Radwanek, Zofia Sendler, Tadeusz
Seweryn, Augusta Szemelowska, Janina Sitko, Andrzej Stopka,
Wincentyna Stopka, Henryk Sosnowski, ks. Witold Stolarczyk,
Kazimierz Sawicki, Fryda Trammer, Karolina Tylko, Maria i Zofia
Włodarczykowie, Stanisław Walczak, Helena Wójcik, Wanda Wójcik,
Anna Wierzbicka, Michał Wierzbicki, Anna Zatorska, Antoni Roman
Zbroja

Those They Carried

Rena Avidar, Janina Altman, Aleksander Allerhand, Anna Allerhand,
Mosze Bejski, Zygmunt Beczkowski, Zygmunt Bernstein, Danuta
Beer, Irena Cynowicz, Józef Dina, Józef Dollinger, Sima Dwir, Janina
Ecker, Jehuda Eisman, Wolf Englender, Anna Etenberg, Moniak
Epsztajn, Chaim Fejler, Sala Feiler, Marcel Fleicher, Fryderyk Gans,
Rosa Geier, Kazimierz Gerkowicz, Icchak szaja Grosman, Frieda
Grosman, Norbert Gruff, Zofia Ginsburg, Miriam Glaser, Aidwa
Goldberg, Helena Goldstein, Aniela Grunberg, Jan Grunberg, Paulina
Grunberg, Ziuta Grunberg, Nina Halpern, Izraela Hargil, Rena
Hausner, Pola Henefeld, Maria Hofman, Monasza Holender, Irena
Honig, Samuel Hochheiser, Borys Ikowicz, Ester Isler, Rena Isler,
Andrzej Jaroszewicz, Edmund Kantor, Helena Kachel, Eda Kunstler,
Rachela Komito, Miriam Korngold, Janina Kon, Józef Kon, Krystyna
Kon, Zbigniew Koszanowski, Ignacy Kraus, Szlomo Leszman, Hanna
Lewinger, Bella Lieber, Jakub Liberman, Joachim Liberman, Józefa
Liberman, Rozalia Neiger, Maria Nowakowska, Lenart Olmer,
Oskar Oliner, Franciszka Oliwa, Chana Orbach, Gustaw Prezl,
Róża Pankowska, Elżbieta Pastor, Maksymilian Perlmutter, Jadwiga
Pempus, Danuta Pempus, Jan Pastor, Felicja Riesel, Lea Riesel, Ida
Ron, Helena Roter, Aszer Rafałowicz, Irena Rajs, Anatol Rabinowicz,
Zofia Rabinowicz, Szoszna Rakowska, Genowefa Rapaport, Stella
Roza, Loen Singer, Nina Silberman, Maria Stefanek, Ewa Silbiger,
Matylda Schneid, Szulim Szapiro, Stella Szczebakowska, Pola
Szechner, Stefan Silbiger, Herman Silberman, Róża Silberman, Lea
Sztainlauf, Leon Sztainlauf, Mordechaj Steinfeld, Elżbieta Taksin,
Lidia Taubelfeld, Jakub Winberg, Nachun Winberg, Stanisława
Wincza, Bronisława Wielfeld, Chana Wiener

Albatross get up,

bless the scales,
bless the strings, good morning.

Albatross rise,
the weight oppresses us, light travels.
A donor bends, conducts, flexes, twists.

Albatross, the waves across the ocean freeze,
bells freeze into sliding boats, ice-shattered,
flap and slide.

I bought you ice-skates, Albatross.
I made you a sailing ship.

Albatross rise—your nesting port is beyond,
light years from resurrection.

When I take your feathered hand,
Albatross of exile, webbed feet bigger
than this space between us, albatross
I bleed.

Breathe, albatross, even the bells
must freeze, your ice-shattered mast
cataracts white.

Albatross, forgive
the mariner, fly

Gravity Prayer

I wear the owl's heart

on my head to know your dreams.

Your face, a cave where ghosts

of my ancestors carved horses

rhinos and the eight-legged lions.

Your wrist, a waist—

of microscopic value.

In barrels we take our thousand years'

sadness

The German media alert civilians about Poles taking sugar from German markets. For a kilo of sugar you pay 5 zl in Poland, but only 2.80 in Germany. *Horror vacui.* Endless processions of Slavs with buckets of sugar. The clouds of white powder. Sugar hovers over herds of Poles. Sweet levitation. Imagine new trades: sugar castles, sugar children's games; sugar erotica; sugar massage therapy; sugar clay; skiing on slopes of sugar. Imagine quicksand of sugar. The festivity of birds gorging on sugar grains.

Poles might think that Germans owe them a bit of sugar, but sugar smuggling runs into a deeper and rather vicious archetype. Sugar came from plantations which gave rise to molasses which gave rise to rum which gave rise to smuggling.

Smugglers were poor people who played at brinksmanship and brought pebbles for seed grain to trouble our shoes. Charles Lamb called a smuggler "the only honest thief." Smuggling is as old as prostitution, but nobler. Adam and Eve were the first smugglers. Smuggling flourished in ancient Carthage. Phoenician merchants smuggled cats to the shores of the eastern Mediterranean Sea and then to Asia where they troubled populations of rodents. Ancient Egyptian law prohibited transporting cats outside of Egypt. Similarly in the 13th century, in England the Government prohibited the international wool trade, but the sheep farmers were saved from this oppression by "owlers," that is to say wool smugglers. Towards the end of the 14th century England had to allow the export of wool. In the 17th century Charles II reintroduced the ban on the export of raw wool. He also declared that every man would be buried in a woolen shroud. Later smuggling shifted from wool to tobacco, tea, and liquor. In 1661 the English Government issued this declaration on smuggling: *A sort of leud people called Smuckellors, never heard of before the late disordered times, who make it their trade … to steal and defraud His Majesty and His Customs.*

Ellis IX

1794 – Massachusetts law called for the return of paupers to their original towns or "to any other place beyond sea where he belongs"

1875 – immigration legislation bars convicts, prostitutes, and coolies

1882 – Chinese immigration is curtailed. Lunatics and idiots sent back

1885 – paupers, polygamists, the insane – excluded

1901 – the owner of the food counter in railroad ticket office was accused of harassing the immigrants

1903 – epileptics, professional beggars, anarchists excluded

1907 – imbeciles, the feeble-minded, tuberculars – excluded

1908 – Robert Watchson, a commissioner of immigration, was forced to resign, as he made immigration soar.

1909 – to raise inspection standards, a commissioner of immigration, William Williams, decided that each immigrant should have at least $25 plus a ticket to his/her destination. The inspection applied this new guideline immediately, even to immigrants who had left Europe before the $25 directive was made public. Over the next eleven days, six hundred and sixty-eight persons were sent back to their ports of departure.

1917 – illiterate excluded. All Japanese excluded

Cancer Ward by Solzhenitsyn was banned. Huxley's *Brave New World* was banned. All Czesław Miłosz's books were banned. At a certain point, Lucy Montgomery was banned. Citizens' thoughts were banned. *Horror vacui.* The establishment banned books which slandered the Soviet Union. As a result, 2,482 books were banned. All the books written on emigration were banned. Books that showed the West as an attractive place. From 1944 to 1945 four-and-a-half million letters were censored. People learned to use a code. If a wife wanted to say her husband was imprisoned for political reasons, she would use certain numbers or write: "he was lately absent." In high school we smuggled quotes from Orwell's *Animal Farm. All animals are equal but some animals are more equal than others.* The noblest contraband dwells in *fraintendimento*, understanding in between.

The hedgehog collects the apples of my mother tongue. He is a dormant god. I take him as my wealth. The hedgehog hunts serpents and hidden thoughts. He protects against evil. Parcels eternity into spiny planets. Each mystery rolls into itself, a thorny crown rolled into a lotus. Leaving, I do not go with empty hands. I carry needles. Violins, stigmas, mulberry seeds. Each thorn a voice of an ancestor. I wear him as a brooch on my shawl. Thorny sun, a fire. For he is the god of suffering under spines. God blessed him with autism. For he is a *Kipod*, a beast of tricks. Defender against serpents and Isidore of Seville. He carries packed eternities into the dusk. As I pass through Customs, it is the hedgehog that smuggles me. My brooch bristles.

Ellis X

Jesus Mary & Joseph where am I?

Split-Second Prayer through Customs

She wraps it up. She hides it. She keeps it under the counter.
She disguises it as white albatross. She keeps vitamins for it.
It hovers above her head. She disguises it as a stone. Cranes
hold little stones in their claws to ward off sleep.
She calls it a hoopoe. She refers to it as evanescence. The Cloud of
Unknowing. In her hands she clasps rosaries. Beads leap
through the space. They fling their seeds in people's faces.
They accrete to the level of their nerves. They undulate.
She smuggles litanies, Saints, epiphanies. There is nobility
in smuggling the same thing over and over again.

Ellis XI

Aliens have no inherent right to land here

Alien races, and foremost those from the Mediterranean, the Orient, and from Slavic countries, are to be met with suspicion, for whatever danger there may be is in the undue preponderance of criminals, the insane, and those becoming public charges. … Immigrants come here at the stage when people are most liable to commit crimes. They are freed from moral restraints and all fear of loss of caste, which, in the lowest order of society, is, next to religion, the strongest deterrent to crime…

—*William Williams*

Both Ellis and Alcatraz at first served as military fortresses.

Both Ellis and Alcatraz have been the setting for crucial parts of the American experience.

2011 Alabama immigration law requires that a foreigner carries a passport and a work permit. Mercedes-Benz executive from Germany arrested in Tuscaloosa, Alabama under the new immigration law for having only his German ID on him.

St. George pierces his spear right through the dragon and kills it. He does not get dirty. St. Michael does not kill the dragon. His spear keeps the dragon at bay. We are unable to eradicate evil. Communism wanted to be like St. George, but ended up perpetuating a new evil. We want to keep evil away from ourselves. We construct fences and walls. We construct borders. We control people's luggage. It is the fear of contamination. Yet, evil smuggles itself in. It is a rhizome. It turns into a grace. Kudzu smuggles itself everywhere. It takes over buildings, churches, telephone poles. It shrouds. It climbs and coils. It spreads over 150,000 acres annually. It is unstoppable. It congregates into worship. It sacrifices its free time for its missionary work. In North Carolina Kudzu covered power utility poles and wires near the town of Kinston into the shape of Christ. Nonnative species colonize our country. Milfoil smuggles itself in water. It grows by rhizomes. It can kill a lake. Its nature is Contraband. Aspen trees smuggle their roots for thousands of acres.

Brass buttons, letters, whispers, prayers, metonymies. In Katyń forest in 1940, more than 14,000 Polish prisoners of war were murdered by the NKVD, the Soviet Secret Police. All in all, the Katyń genocide harvested 21,000 deaths of Polish officers, intelligentsia, clerics, and officials. They were shot in the back of the head and thrown into mass graves. For 50 years, the Soviets covered this up, blaming it on the Nazis. There was no mention of Katyń in newspapers, books, textbooks. People who spoke the truth were incarcerated. Only brass buttons and saints witnessed.

Emergency Prayer

It comes in a veil, it waits
under a black chador. It churns
up grains, tides, whispers

Its feet are wounded, dark
banished nests. Stitched
wings of owls

Crucifixions are light
years away from resurrections

Death perches in a fog
San Miniato carries his head
across the river

It is the length of a toddler

March 1940. Stalin lapdog, Beria, types
the liquidation documents
14,700 prisoners of war,
11,000 other prisoners
to be wiped out from the earth

Dogwood grows in silence

A fog rises from the dead,
orphans the chairs

21,000 swallows, the geometry
of crosses

The trees in Katyń—red
relics, candles, cranes at dusk
Infrared incisions ghost rays

Pentimento

Their backs—cradles
Oysters sealed up

The true annunciation happens
in the dark—

It empties the chairs,
It sits on a camphor tree

Buttons from coats and uniforms
wedding rings
brass buttons
pieces of a rosary
buttons
a letter from a child
a letter from a wife
buttons
medallions
scapulars

A father and his son on the same death
list. *Wsie rowno*, the officer says.
The father goes. He leaves for his son
a Madonna he drew in the wood

The Virgin is a small wizened girl
with shrunken halo
She carries eternity
in her walls

Her veil will lift once a week
To reveal an icon

In the clouds, in branches
In this blue *Mandorla*

a Polycandela

The whole forest lit

with blue gas rooms
Death comes in a veil, it waits under
a black chador. It churns up grains
of tides and whispers—

On a branch it perches, on an invisible stretcher—

It sits on a log and pounds
it is a drumming station—

It sits on a log and pounds its wings
the dogwood hears

Ellis XII

What's your skill? Occupation?

How much money do you have?

Are you single?

Are you married?

Can you draw a diamond?

How do you wash stairs? From the top or the bottom?

My mother meets me in a Manhattan apartment
with her collection:
a rug that looks like grass,
happy birthday clock,
a picture frame: "just about to be married,"
age-defying cream,
a set of silver Christmas salad tongs,
four packs of cards
with Hoyle's rules,
water shoes.

All of it a beautiful chance meeting of a sewing machine with an umbrella.
I compress them into my backpack, disparate
elements of her life. Each object, a bead of her rosary.
I am to smuggle them across the States.

I will meet her when the morning meets the meadow. I will sing of
Trobrianders. Of a shoe in a boutonniere. My throat tips are ink-
stained.

In Poland where she grew up, the magpies collect all the jewelry.
The storks align themselves on the houses. Their nests, the lighthouses
of returns. Their bills, postmarked pillage.

Back in Krowica on the border of Ukraine I walk
from a house to a cemetery.
I pass a horse in the garden and chickens greet me under the awnings,
I visit the well into which my brother threw a cat—

The storks align themselves on the roofs. The apparitions
of black and white Madonnas with long legs.

On my grandmother's grave, I examine the letters.
There are chicks pacing up and down the rooms of her childhood.
I cannot pack them. I cannot pack the storks. The silence of the dead.
Only pilgrims are true smugglers
and hummingbirds who meticulously calculate their rates of return.

Wherever we are, we pack things.
It is only the gravity of objects that keeps us from moving.

The hoopoe is a solitary bird yet has enormous filial devotion. When the parents of the hoopoe grow old, the young hoopoe will preen his parents' feathers and lick their eyes until they become young again. Therefore the hoopoe smuggles them into the realm of the eternal. The hoopoe dances and brings more dung to its nest. If any bird showed himself truly, with all faults and failures, wouldn't that be more beautiful than hiding behind the myriads of feathers, layers of beaks and the shriek sounds of the night in them? But who is the One who smuggles the hoopoe? Who is the One who redeems each fallen feather that turns into seconds and minutes drifting into air? Who is behind all the "imping"? Is our soul involved in the hoopoe dispatch? What kind of diplomacy is required to smuggle the self into Infinity?

Customs Declaration Prayer

I take spots of time.
They live in my synapses.
You cannot declare them.
Check the pulse of the air.
I take these trees, heavy with
clumps of green and celestial swelling.
With single notes of mystery.
I hang kisses on them which orbit their girth.
Synapses and quarks fleck the sky.
The grass the air the phlox.
We could leap words to count the routes
of their returns. Lift two thousand bee balms,
bleeding hearts and foxgloves to the light.
Splashers of transparency. At the tip of the air,
feel the apparition of its heartbeat.

Between you and me, a tree takes root,
a bird rages in its hollows,
devastates its dark,
steals the seeds of

These filthy immigrants are sewing tuberculosis into my clothes

Ellis XIII

Commissioner William Williams writes to President Theodore Roosevelt:

The evil features of the present immigration cannot be reached by the mere enactment of further specific disabilities such as illiteracy. Even with the proposed new disability foreigners will continue to pour into this country whose presence will tend to lower our standard of living and civilization.

Nov 25th, 1902

But now there came multitudes of men of the lowest class from the south of Italy and men of the meaner sort out of Hungary and Poland, men of the ranks where there was neither skill nor energy nor any initiative of quick intelligence; and they came in numbers which increased from year to year, as if the countries of the south of Europe were disburdening themselves of the more hapless elements of their population.

Ellis XIV

What did Alcatraz inmates leave in their cells:
a black handball, a baseball with initials written in blood
a pack of Kool cigarettes, a whistle, a boat schedule
Robert Stroud left birds

What did the Orchard Street tenements leave:

Levin Harry and Jenny left:

a Chinese laundry certificate, buckwheat grain
a beet stein, a jar, synthetic cooking fat, tools
for sewing, an 1897 calendar on the wall

Rogshefsky Fanny & Abraham left:

candle sticks, wooden weights

The Moore family left:

Agnes Moore who died
at the age of 1 from swill milk.
Windows were left open to let her
spirit out

Katz Ben (1930) left:

a toothbrush,
combs for lice
milk tops
a shampoo bottle
a signature on the wall

Prayer

I leave stones of ripples
my mouth spits out oaks, *kora*, ancient rituals,
milk from St. Mary's breast, a crest of a hoopoe,

A tulip tree, yellow birch, eye-salmon rose
fiddlehead ferns, ruffed grouse, a flock of

enunciations

ingrate spoiled insulated

Now, a shower after shower
a *gestu* after *gestu*
shindig after shindig

Mouth taps iron ghosts
bark means *kora*
keeps burning till
it brains forth

Between country and country, crocuses grow.
Do not regret a crocus when woods are on fire.

The storks align themselves with the lighthouses.
Hummingbirds calculate rates of return.

Between us a *memorare* of raw sea-weed

Left
with a poem in my mouth,
a sphere a curled hedgehog
prickly calm inexhaustible

The desire for hooks in the wall

Hoopoe smuggles Spring and gratitude. Hoopoe smuggles death, cemeteries, cemeteries and death, spring of death, death and spring, spring & death & gratitude of death. Spring of gratitude. Hoopoe smuggles the hoopoe. Hoopoe is the dybbuk. Hoopoe smuggles dybbuks. The dybbuk smuggles a hoopoe. "So long as we do not die to ourselves, and so long as we identify with someone or something, we shall never be free," says the Hoopoe. "The spiritual way is not for those wrapped up in exterior life," says the hoopoe. "For how can you remain the master of yourself if you follow your likes and dislikes?" says the hoopoe. Smuggling is wrapped up in exteriors. Smuggling has to transgress itself. Smuggling is the way of the parrot. "Set up upon your Way, for you are not an almond you are only the shell," says the Hoopoe to the parrot. "In this vast ocean the world is an atom and the atom a world. Who knows which is of more value here, the cornelian or the pebble?" says the hoopoe. "How is it that I see not the hoopoe, or is he among the absent?" says the Prophet Sulayman in *Surah al-Naml*, in the Holy Quran (27:20). Hoopoe is an invisible one. Hoopoe is always in progress. There is no progression without the hoopoe.

Customs:

We take the turf   **15**
To thy high requiem become a sod – Keats' "Ode to a Nightingale" (lines 59-60).

All the Ellis poems sprang from my visits to Ellis Island and The Tenement Museum in NY, as well as several books on immigration: *Ellis Island Immigration's Shining Center,* John T. Cummingham *Ellis Island Portraits 1905-1920,* Augustus F. Sherman *97 Orchard,* Jane Ziegelman

We are hordes of Tartar cheeks   **19**
Inspired by *Travels of Marco Polo.*

Hoopoe Poem   **20**
The reference to Sufi mystic, Simurgh, and various birds' attachments originate in the Sufi epic *Conference of Birds* by Attar.

Smuggling's disruption   **21**
The reference to Joyce comes from James Gavin's "Bloomsday, 2011" | James Joyce, Class Warrior http://owlsmag.wordpress.com/category/project-blooms-baskets/. References to Emily Dickinson come from the objects and fascicles kept at the Emily Dickinson Archive at Amherst College.

There is no life for them   **22**
The grey doves in your many branches code and decode what warnings? – Robert Duncan's "Doves"

Jan Karski   **24**
A Pole, a member of the Polish underground and a courier during World War II. He would disguise himself as a Jew in order to get into the ghetto and carry the evidence of the Nazi crimes to the powerful world leaders (called by Karski "the Lords of Humanity"), such as Roosevelt, in order to stop the Holocaust. After his meeting with Roosevelt, a small note in the *NY Times* appeared merely on the 16th page. On May 29, 2012, Jan Karski received a posthumous Presidential Medal of Freedom awarded by President Barack Obama. There is also a documentary in the progress of making by Sławomir Grünberg: *Karski & the Lords of Humanity.*

It hides in between the birches   **26**
the chinks in the forest from Auden

Those They Carried   **60**
Names of saved Jews come from an exhibition on the *Righteous* which
opened on November 5, 2013 in the Museum Factory of Oskar Schindler,
part of the Kraków Historical Museum.

The exhibition also presents the following documents:

A street poster in *Częstochowa September 1942:*
*Any person who provides shelter to Jews, supplies them with food or sells it to
them is subject to the death penalty.*

Street announcement, November 19, 1942, Przemyśl:
*Each Pole or Ukrainian attempting to help a Jew is subject to the death penalty.
The punishment applies as well to all those who fail to notify the police about any
one hiding Jews.*

Smugglers were poor people   **64**
Quoted from *The Compleat Smuggler: A Book About Smuggling In England,
America and Elsewhere, Past and Present* by Jefferson Farjeon.

Ellis X   **68**
The first words of a Polish Immigrant in the 1900s after arriving on Ellis
Island.

Ellis XI   **70**
In 2011, the Ellis Island Museum featured an Alcatraz Exhibition.
*Both Ellis and Alcatraz have been the setting for crucial parts of the American
experience* - Michael Bloomberg, the Office of the Mayor, City of NY.

Emergency Prayer   **73**
The reference is to the genocide in Katyń where in 1940 the Soviets
murdered 21,000 Polish officers, clerics, and officials.
The line *Fog rises from the dead* is an allusion to the April 2011 airplane
crash in Smoleńsk, where Polish president Kaczyński and 90 other
government officials meant to land to commemorate the Katyń genocide.

Ellis XII   **77**
The interrogation questions posed to Immigrants arriving on Ellis Island
come from the Ellis Island Museum.

These filthy immigrants   **82**
Information about the sweat shops and the treatment of the immigrants
living on 97 Orchard Street was obtained from my visit to the Tenement
Museum in New York in 2011.

Ellis XIII   83

Notes are from the Ellis Island Museum as well as from Woodrow
Wilson's book *A History of the American People* (1901).

Ellis XIV   84

Information about tenants living on 97 Orchard Street in NY and
the objects that survived them comes from my visits to the Tenement
Museum. Information about Alcatraz inmates comes from my visit to
Alcatraz.

Acknowledgments:

Grateful acknowledgment is made to *Jubilat* which published and featured online "Sausage Poem" (including the video recording of it), as well as the editors of the following publications, in which individual Contraband poems first appeared, or are forthcoming:

Anthem Journal
The Café Review
Eleven Eleven
Fraza (in Poland)
Laurel Review
Spoon River Review
Squaw Valley Review
Storyscape
Others will Enter the Gates: Immigrant Poets on Poetry, Influences, and Writing in America, Black Lawrence Press, 2015

I am honored and grateful that Rusty Morrison, the editor of Omnidawn Publishing, embraced these poems as well as helped and encouraged me in the revision process.

I am grateful to Squaw Valley Community Writers during whose summer workshops with Kazim Ali, Dean Young, Lucille Clifton, Evie Shockley, C. D. Wright, Forrest Gander, Robert Hass, Brenda Hillman, Sharon Olds, some of these poems emerged.

Grateful thanks to Zachary Finch, Teresa Cader, Tony Brinkley, Rita Simmonds, Eric DeLuca, Ivy T. Schweitzer and Julie Püttgen for their insights, inspirations, and revision comments.

I also want to thank my fellow poets from two poetry groups: Jeff Friedman, Jennifer Militello, Ivy T. Schweitzer, Lisa Solberg Furmanski, Giavanna Munafo, Nancy J. Crumbine, Jane Ackerman, Marissa Miller. Without their suggestions and encouragement this work would be impoverished.

Separate thanks to Mary Jo Bang for her wise council and directions.

Finally, "illegal" and playful thanks to all the smugglers and immigrants who shared their stories with me, as well as to my dad Michał Chruściel who has been an endless source of history classes and smuggling stories under the regime of Stalinism and Communism in Poland.

Ewa Chrusciel and hoopoe. Photograph by Urszula Lukaszuk.

Ewa Chrusciel has two books in Polish: *Furkot* and *Sopiłki* and one book in English, *Strata*, which won the 2009 International Book Contest and was published with Emergency Press in 2011. Her poems were featured in *Jubilat, Boston Review, Colorado Review, Lana Turner, Spoon River Review,* and *Aufgabe,* among others. She translated Jack London, Joseph Conrad, and I.B. Singer, as well as a number of contemporary American poets, into Polish. She is an associate professor at Colby-Sawyer College.

Contraband of Hoopoe
by Ewa Chrusciel

Cover text set in Kabel LT Std.
Interior text set in Adobe Caslon Pro, Joanna MT Std, & Kabel LT Std.

Cover art: Julie Püttgen, *Cloudmapping: Conference of the Birds*, 2008.
Gouache, watercolor, and pencil, 12 × 16 inches

Cover & interior design by Cassandra Smith

Offset printed in the United States
by Edwards Brothers Malloy, Ann Arbor, Michigan
On 55# Enviro Natural 100% Recycled 100% PCW
Acid Free Archival Quality FSC Certified Paper
with Rainbow FSC Certified Colored End Papers

Omnidawn Publishing
Richmond, California
2014
Rusty Morrison & Ken Keegan, Senior Editors & Publishers
Gillian Hamel, Managing Poetry Editor & *OmniVerse* Managing Editor
Cassandra Smith, Poetry Editor & Book Designer
Peter Burghardt, Poetry Editor & Book Designer
Turner Canty, Poetry Editor
Liza Flum, Poetry Editor & Social Media
Sharon Osmond, Poetry Editor & Bookstore Outreach
Pepper Luboff, Poetry Editor & Feature Writer
Juliana Paslay, Fiction Editor & Bookstore Outreach Manager
Gail Aronson, Fiction Editor
RJ Ingram, Social Media
Melissa Burke, Poetry Editor & Feature Writer
Sharon Zetter, Grant Writer & Poetry Editor